EASY PIANO

STRANGER THINGS

MUSIC FROM THE NETFLIX ORIGINAL SERIES

CONTENTS:

ISBN: 978-1-70517-945-1

Hal•Leonard®

7777 W. Bluemound Rd. P.O. Box 13819 Milwaukee, WI 53213

Visit Hal Leonard Online at
www.halleonard.com

World headquarters, contact:
Hal Leonard
7777 West Bluemound Road
Milwaukee, WI 53213
Email: info@halleonard.com

In Europe, contact:
Hal Leonard Europe
1 Red Place
London, W1K 6PL
Email: info@halleonardeurope.com

In Australia, contact:
Hal Leonard Australia Pty. Ltd.
4 Lentara Court
Cheltenham, Victoria, 3192 Australia
Email: info@halleonard.com.au

THE GHOST IN YOU

Words and Music by RICHARD BUTLER
and TIM BUTLER

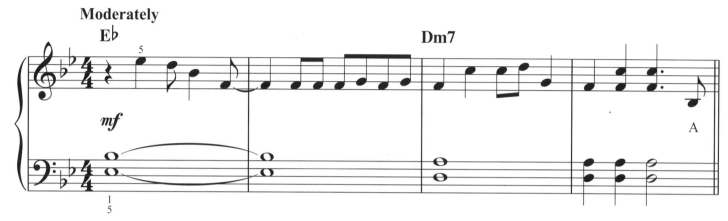

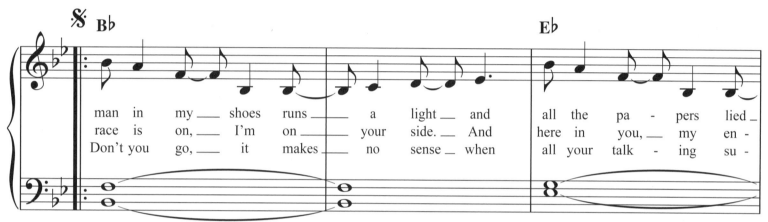

man in my ___ shoes runs ___ a light ___ and
race is on, ___ I'm on ___ your side. ___ And
Don't you go, ___ it makes ___ no sense ___ when

all the pa - pers lied
here in you, ___ my en -
all your talk - ing su -

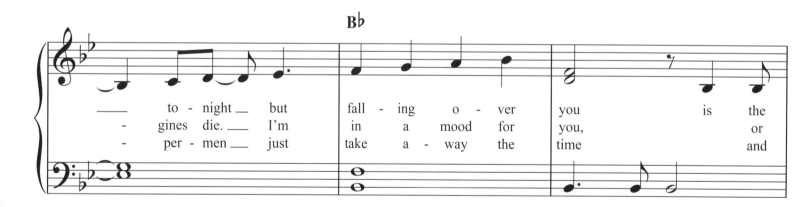

___ to - night ___ but
- gines die. ___ I'm
- per - men ___ just

fall - ing o - ver
in a mood for
take a - way the

you ___ is the
you, ___ or
time ___ and

news of the day.
run - ning a - way.
get in the way.

An - gels
Stars come
Ain't it

Eb(add2)　　　Dm7　　　　　　　　Eb(add2)

fall　　like　　rain,＿＿＿＿　　and　love,　love,
down　　in　　you,＿＿＿＿　　and　love,　love,
just　　like　　rain?＿＿＿＿　And　love,　love,

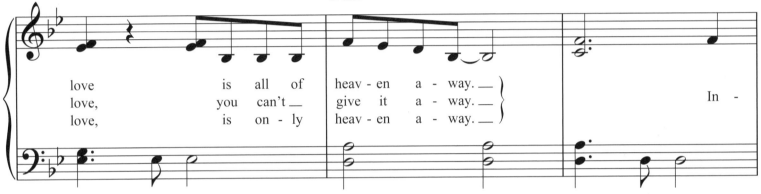

Dm7

love　　　　is　all　of　heav-en　a-way.＿
love,　　　you　can't＿give　it　a-way.＿
love,　　　is　on-ly　heav-en　a-way.＿

In -

F　　　　　　　　　　　　　　Eb

side　you＿　the　time　moves,＿　and　she　don't＿　fade.

F　　　　　　　　　　Eb(add2)

The　ghost　in＿＿　you,　she　don't＿　fade.＿＿

4

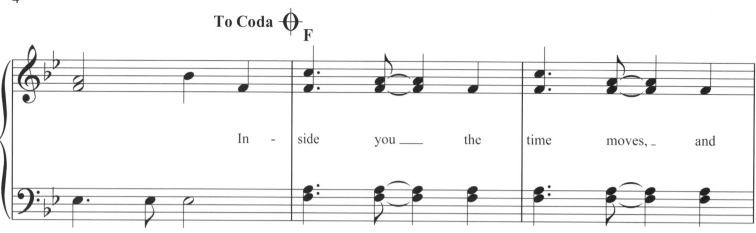

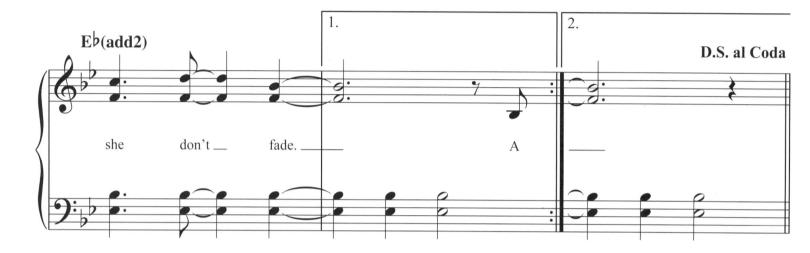

AFRICA

Words and Music by DAVID PAICH
and JEFF PORCARO

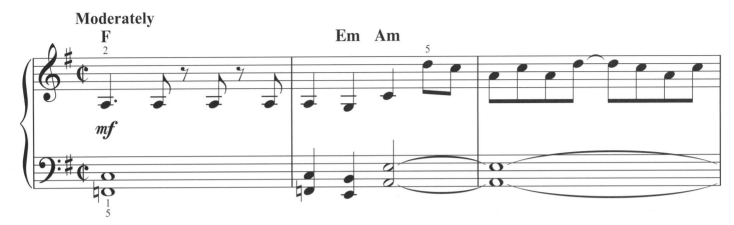

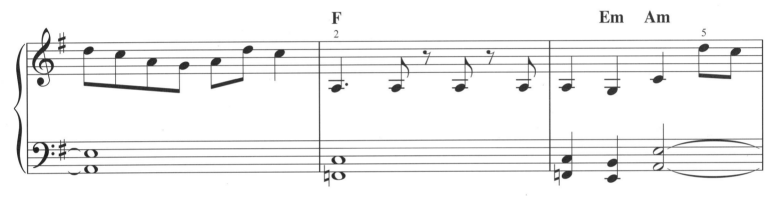

I hear the drums

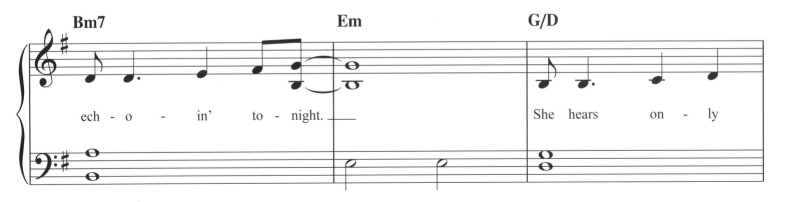

ech- o - in' to - night. ___   She hears on - ly

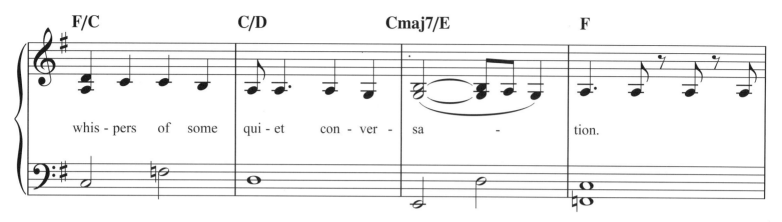

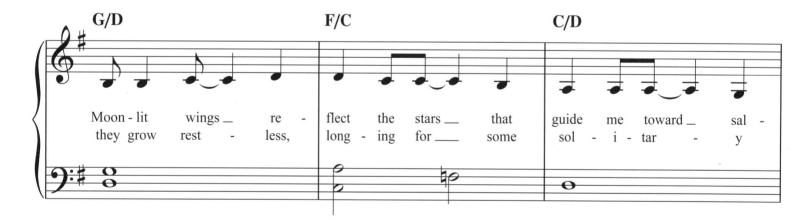

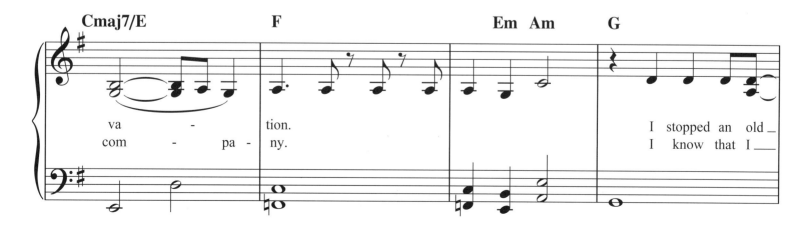

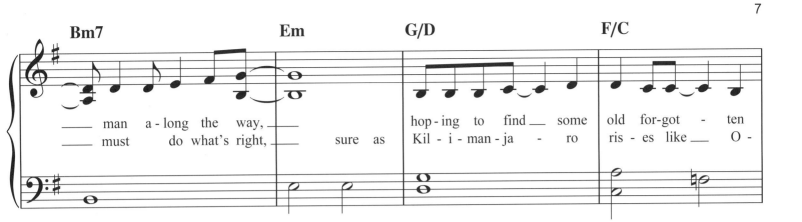

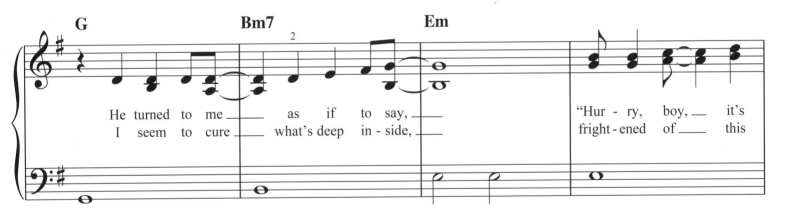

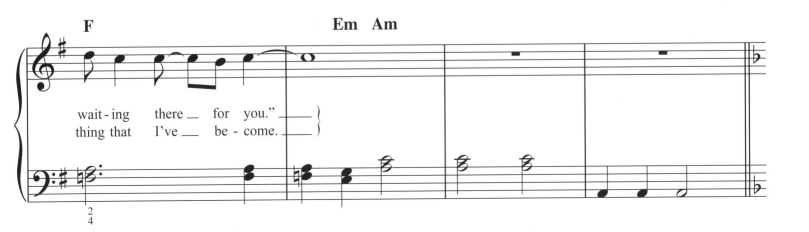

It's gon-na take a lot to drag — me a-way — from you. —

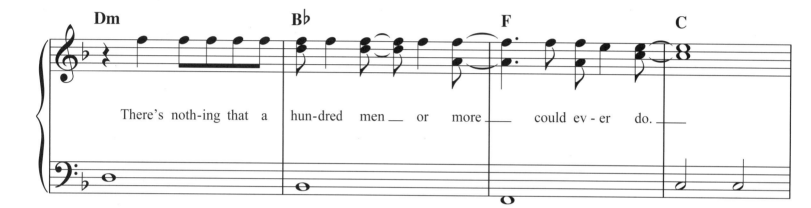

There's noth-ing that a hun-dred men — or more — could ev - er do. —

I bless the rains — down in Af - ri - ca. —

Gon-na take some time to do — the things we nev - er had. —

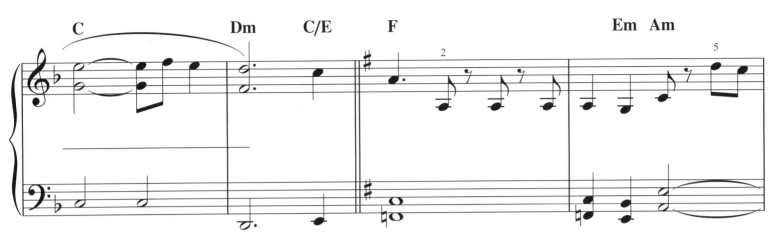

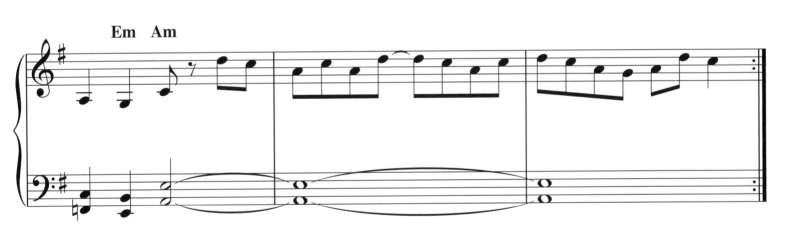

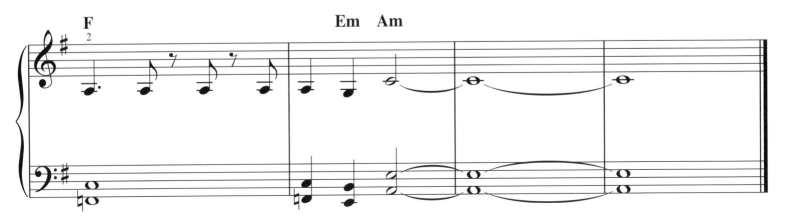

COLD AS ICE

Words and Music by MICK JONES
and LOU GRAMM

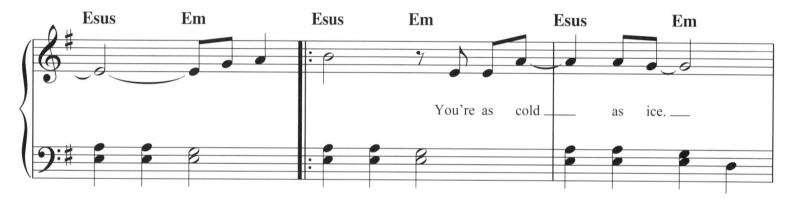

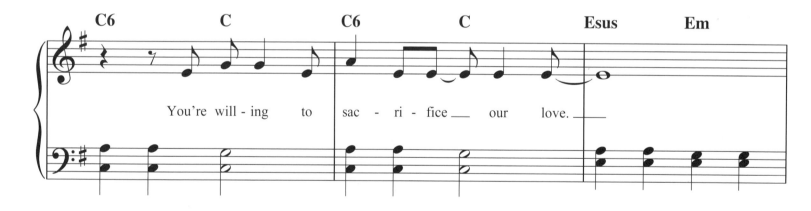

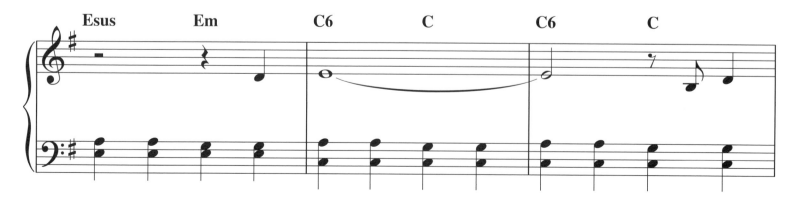

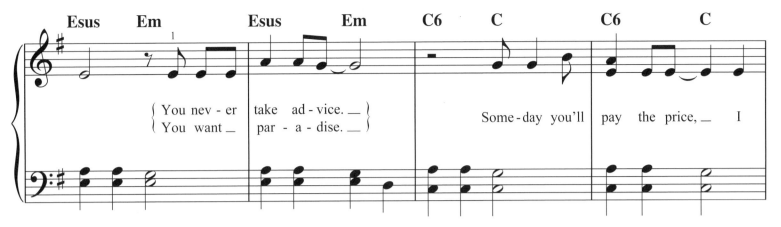

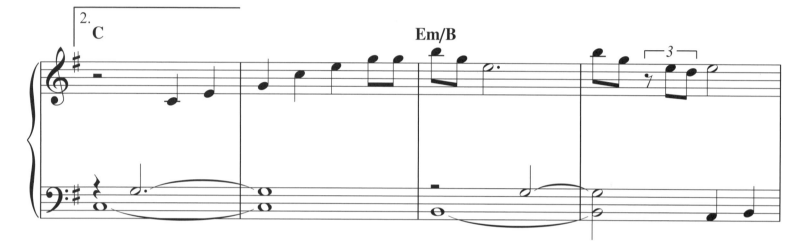

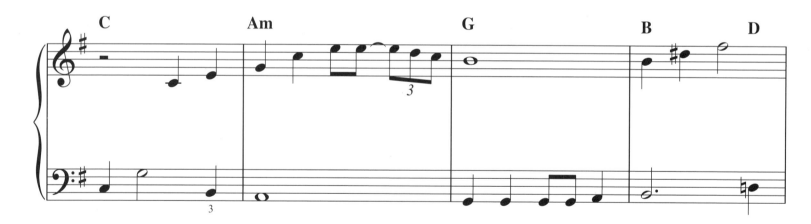

Cold   as   ice.   You know _____ that you are.

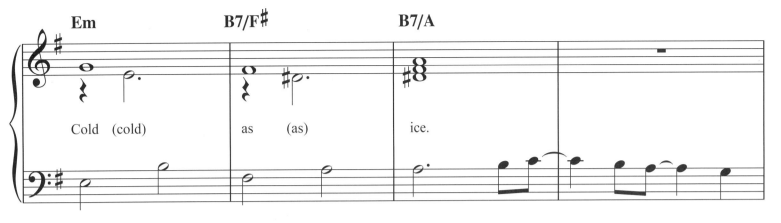

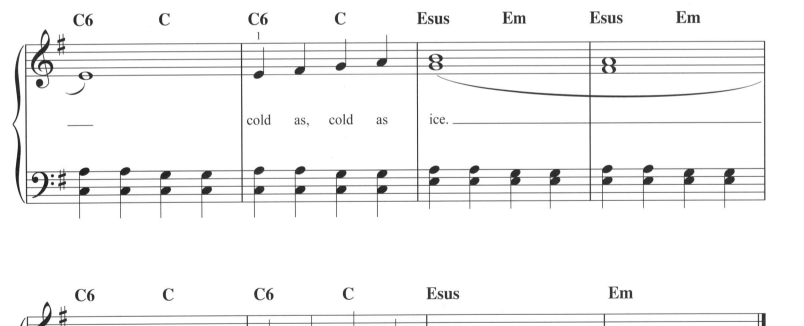

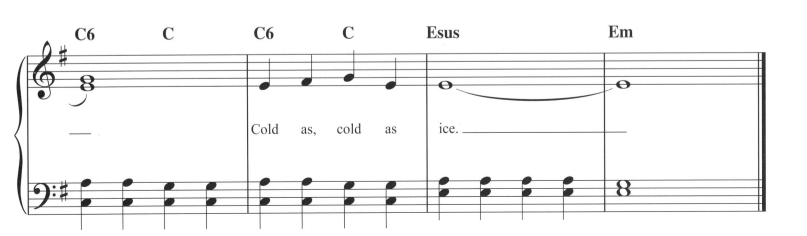

ELEVEN

By KYLE DIXON
and MICHAEL STEIN

Moderately, with expression

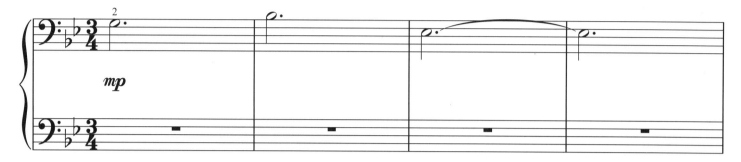

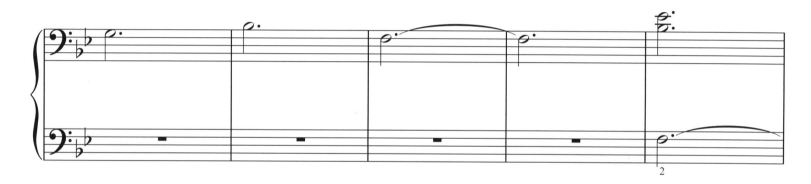

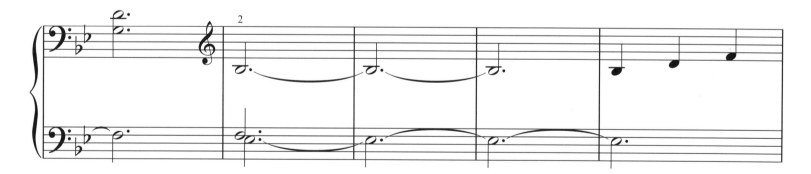

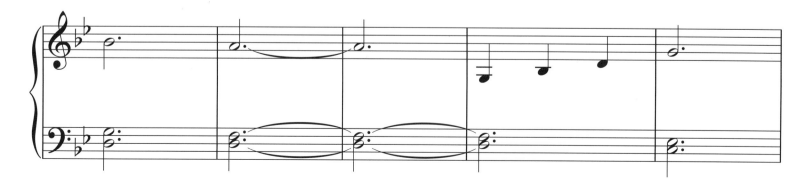

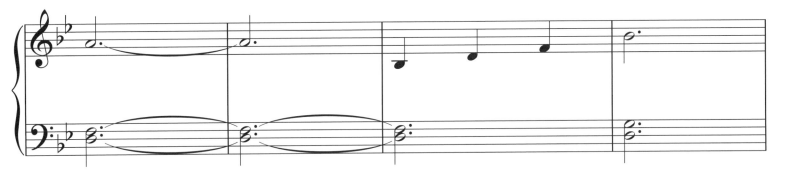

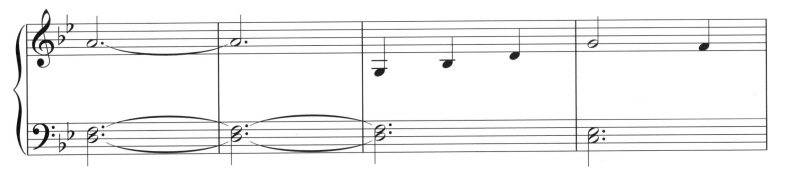

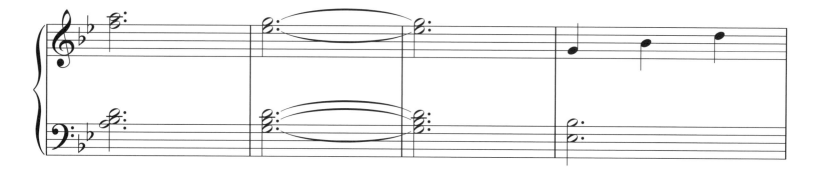

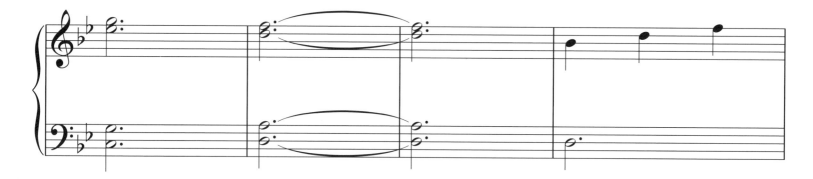

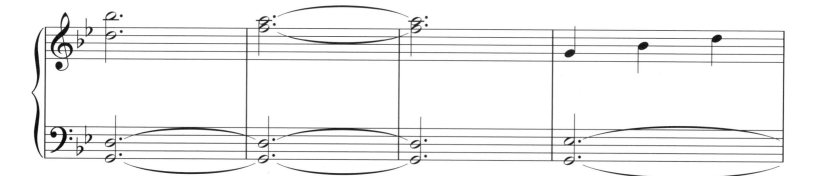

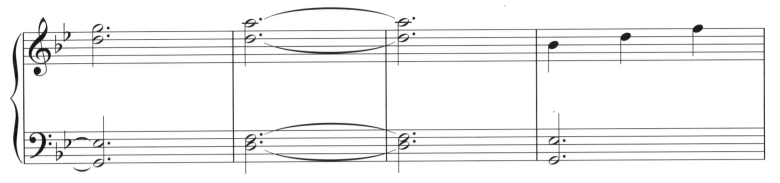

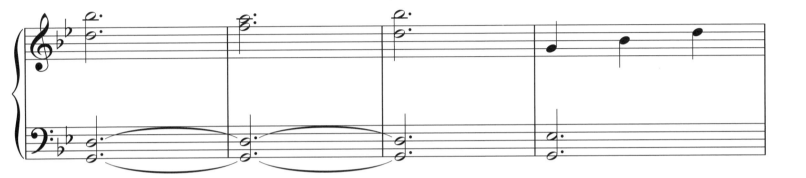

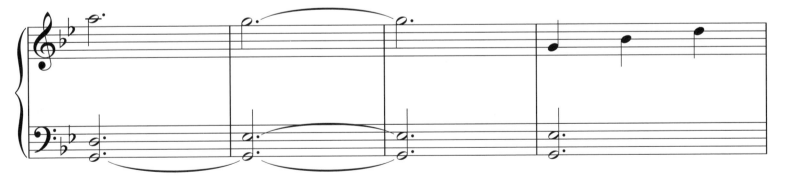

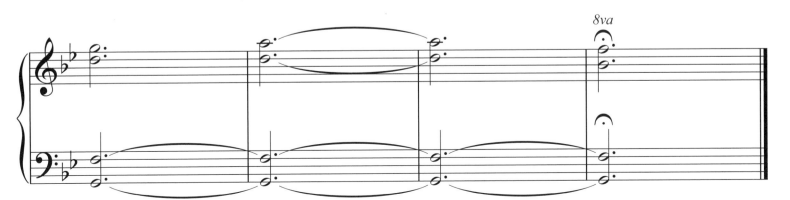

LOVERGIRL

Words and Music by
MARY C. BROCKERT

Moderate Dance groove

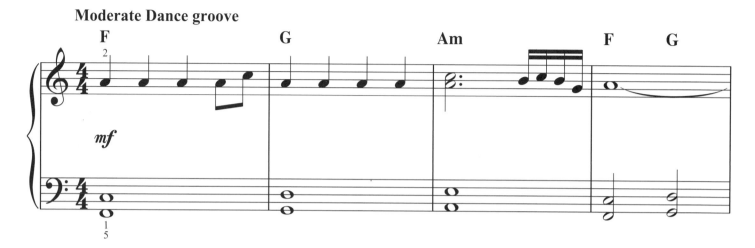

Cof - fee, tea or me, ba - by, tou - ché o - lé.
Hook, line and sink - er, ba - by, that's how you caught me.

My op - 'ning line might be a bit pas - sé, ___ yes. But don't think that I don't know what
My sec - ond verse might be a bit old hat. ___ But, ___ don't think that I don't know what

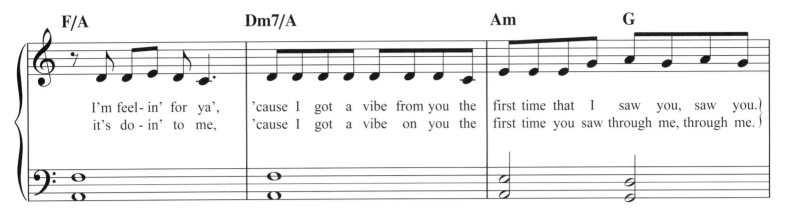

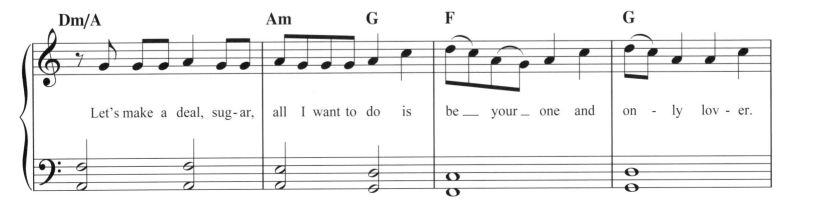

20

I just want to be your lov - er - girl. _____

I just want to rock your world. _____

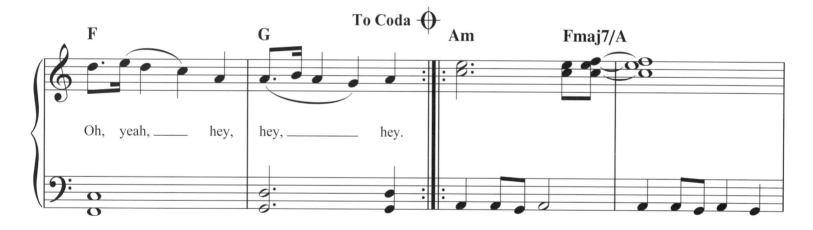

Oh, yeah, _____ hey, hey, _____ hey.

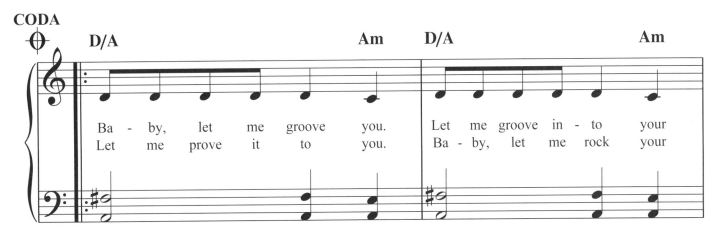

CODA

Baby, let me groove you.
Let me prove it to you.

Let me groove in-to your
Ba - by, let me rock your

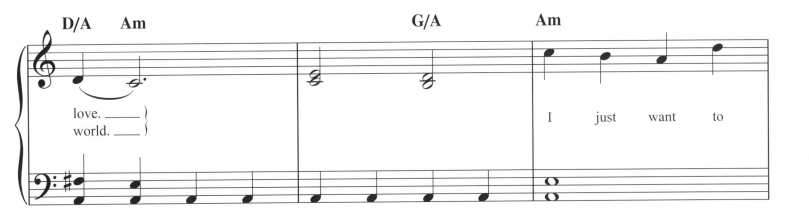

love. _____
world. _____

I just want to

be your lov - er - girl. _____

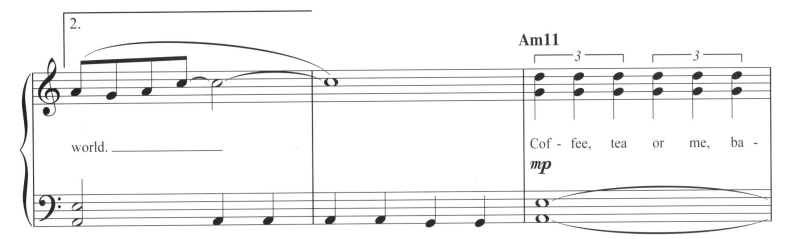

world. _____

Cof - fee, tea or me, ba -

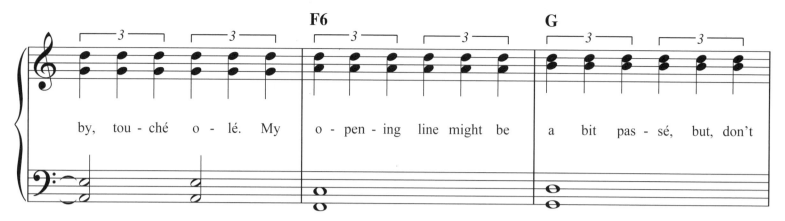

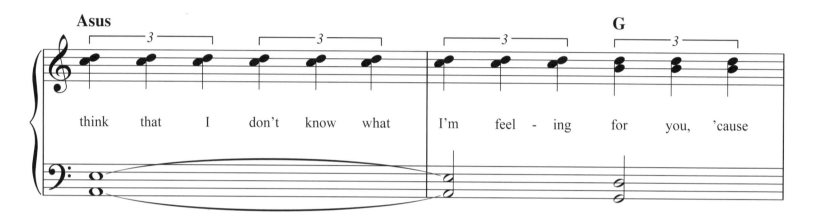

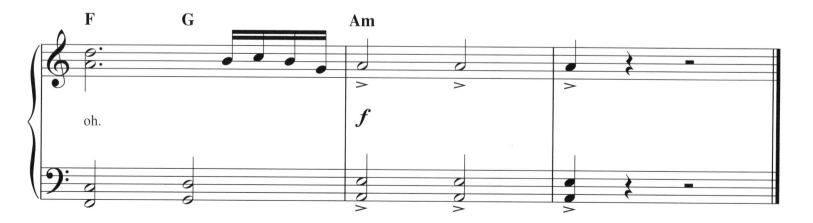

EVERY BREATH YOU TAKE

Music and Lyrics by
STING

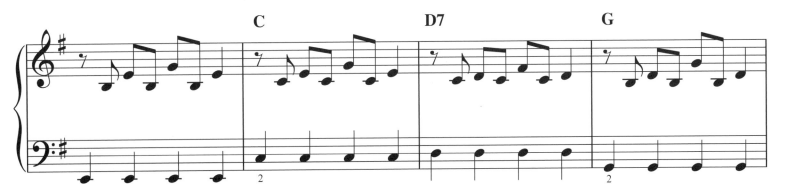

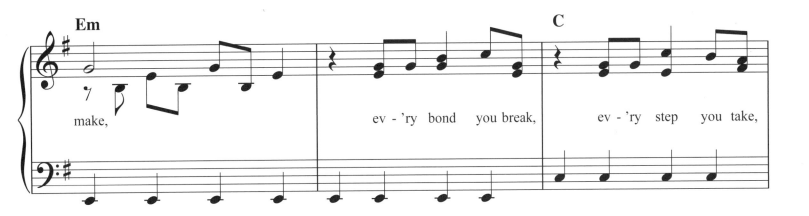

I'll be watch-ing you.

Ev - 'ry sin - gle ___

day,

ev - 'ry word you ___ say,

ev - 'ry game you play,

ev - 'ry night you stay,

I'll be watch-ing you.

Oh, can't you ___ see

you be-long to

me? How my poor heart _ aches _____ with ev-'ry step _ you

take. Ev-'ry move you __ make,

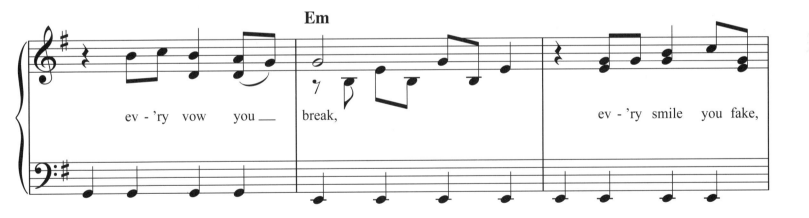

ev-'ry vow you __ break, ev-'ry smile you fake,

ev-'ry claim you stake, I'll be watch-ing you.

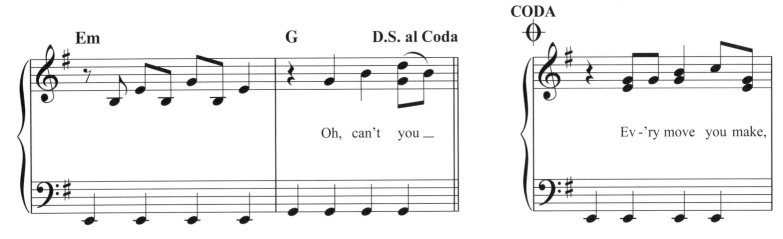

KIDS

By KYLE DIXON
and MICHAEL STEIN

MASTER OF PUPPETS

Words and Music by JAMES HETFIELD,
LARS ULRICH, KIRK HAMMETT
and CLIFF BURTON

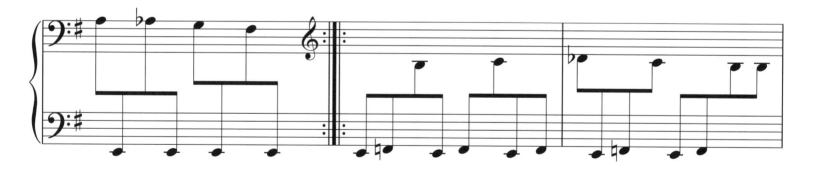

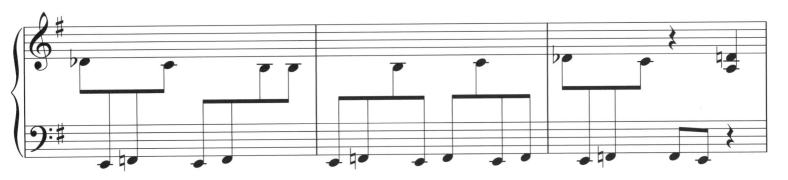

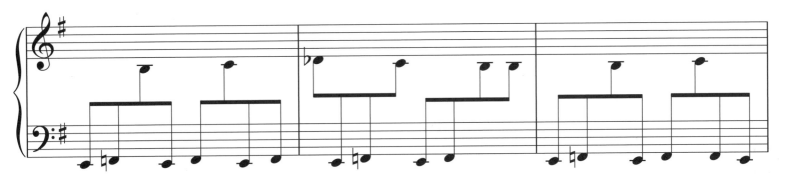

End of pas - sion play, crum - bl - ing a - way,
Nee - dle - work _ the way, nev - er you be - tray,
Hell is worth _ all that, nat - 'ral hab - i - tat, _

— I'm your source _ of self - de - struc -
— life or death _ be - com - ing clear -
— just a rhyme _ with - out a rea -

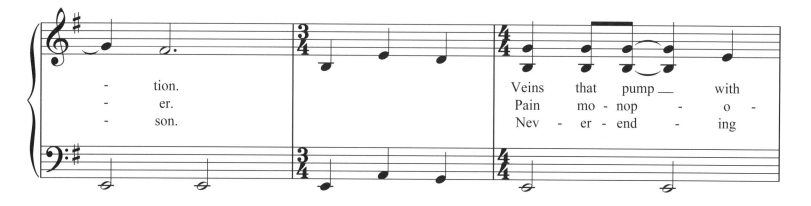

- tion. Veins that pump _ with
- er. Pain mo - nop - o - o -
- son. Nev - er - end - ing

fear, suck - ing dark - est clear,
ly, rit - ual mis - er - y,
maze, drift on num - bered days,

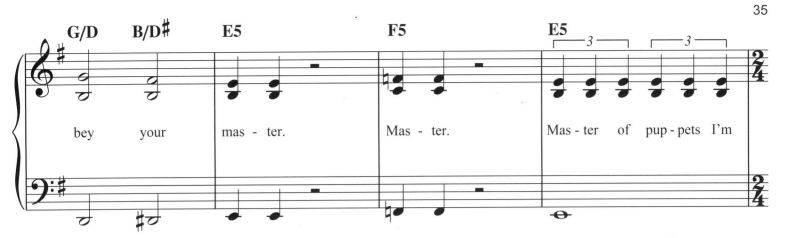

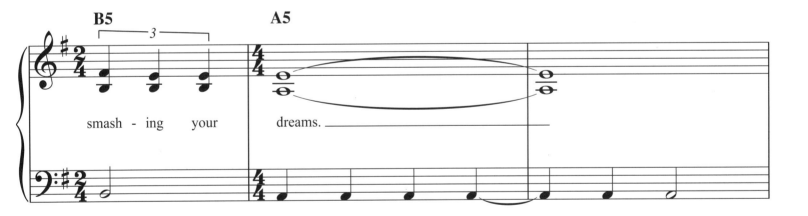

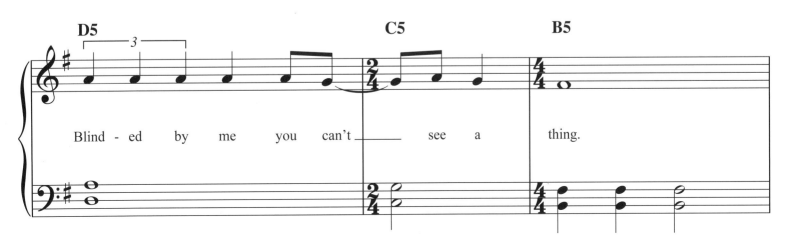

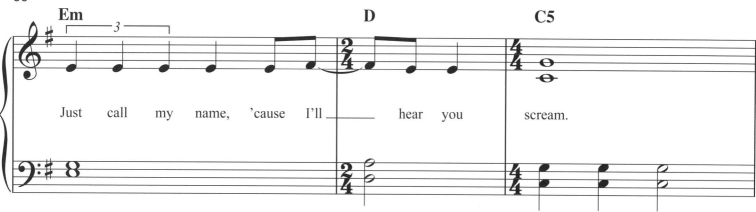

Just call my name, 'cause I'll ___ hear you scream.

Mas - ter. Mas - ter. Just say my name, 'cause I'll ___

___ hear you scream. ___ Mas - ter.

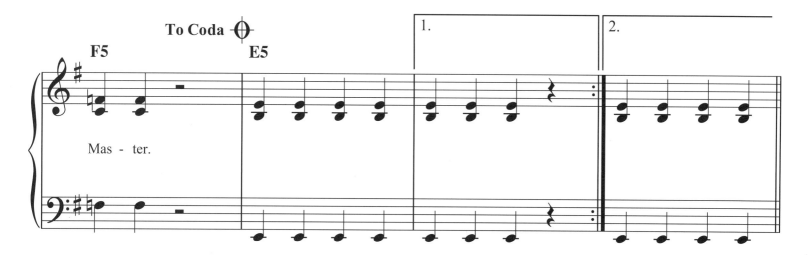

To Coda

1.

2.

Mas - ter.

NEUTRON DANCE

Words and Music by DANNY SEMBELLO
and ALLEE WILLIS

Moderately fast

I don't want to take it an-y-more.
There's no mon-ey fall-ing from the sky
In-dus-try don't pay a price that's fair,

'cause a   I'll   just   stay   here   locked   be - hind   the
all the   com - mon   peo - ple   breath - ing   filth - y

door.   Just   no   time   to
blind.   Some - one stole   my
air.   Roof caved in   on

stop and get a - way   'cause   I
brand new Chev - ro - let,   and   the
all the sim - ple dreams,   and   to

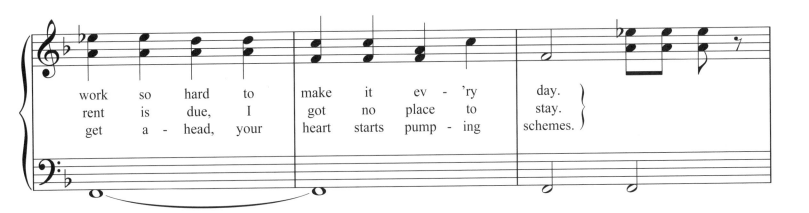

work so hard to   make it ev - 'ry   day.
rent is due, I   got no place to   stay.
get a - head, your heart starts pump - ing schemes.

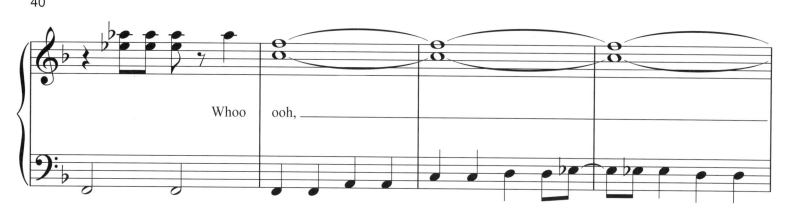

Whoo ooh, _____

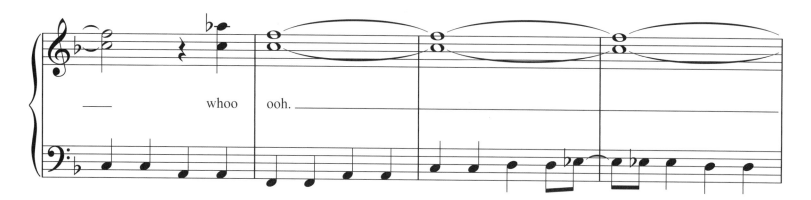

_____ whoo ooh. _____

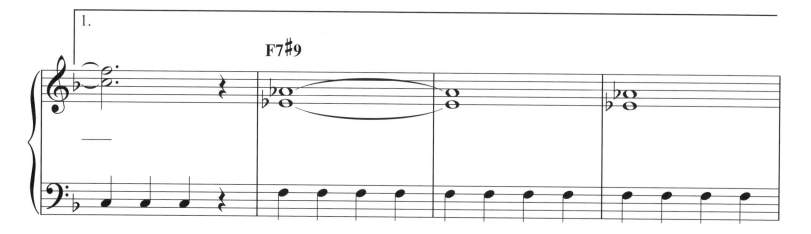

1.

F7♯9

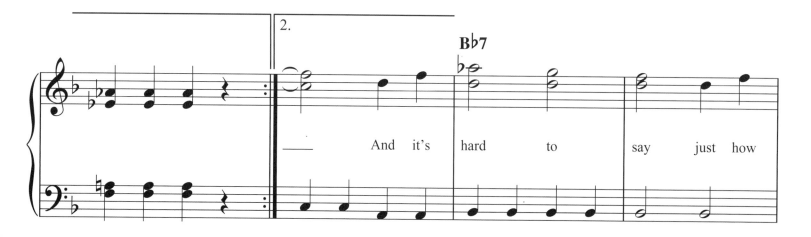

2.

B♭7

_____ And it's hard to say just how

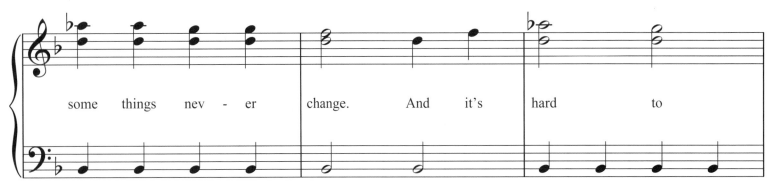

some things nev - er change. And it's hard to

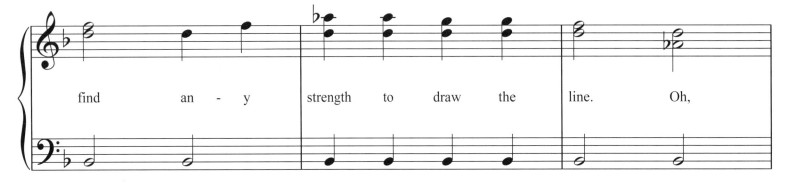

find an - y strength to draw the line. Oh,

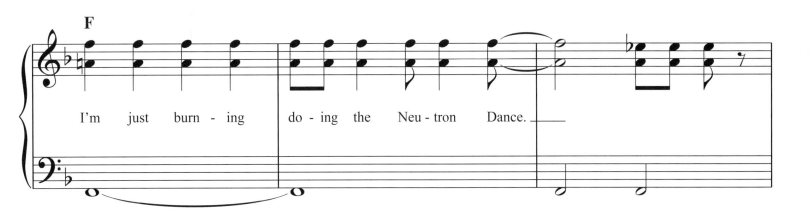

I'm just burn - ing do - ing the Neu - tron Dance. __

I'm just burn - ing do - ing the Neu - tron Dance. _

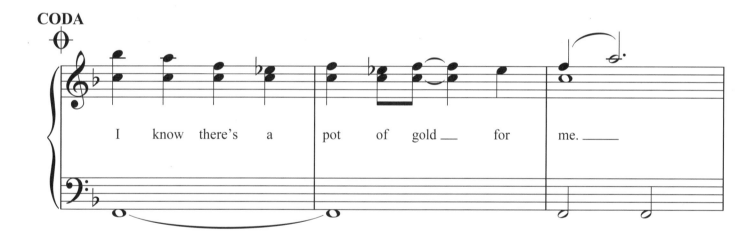

I know there's a pot of gold ___ for me. ___

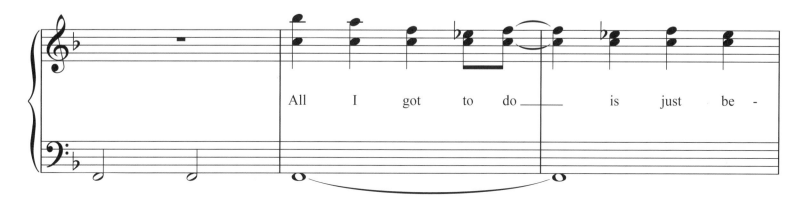

All I got to do ___ is just be -

NEVER SURRENDER

Words and Music by
COREY HART

Moderately

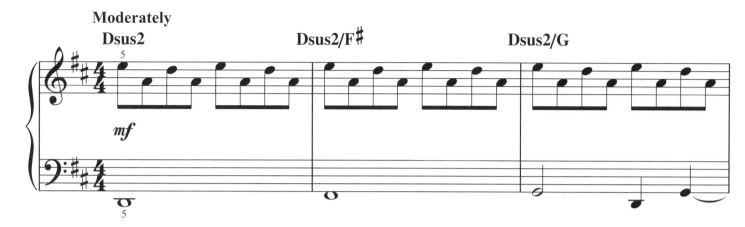

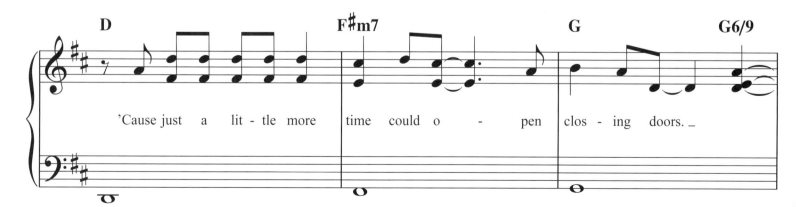

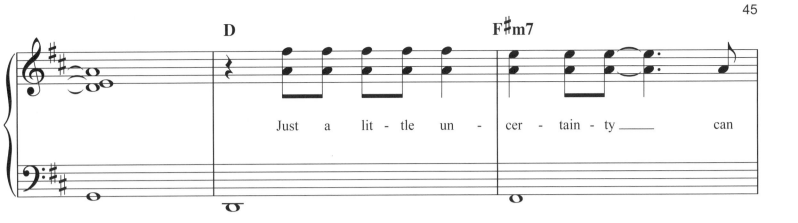

Just a lit - tle un - cer - tain - ty _____ can

bring you down. _ And no - bod - y wants to

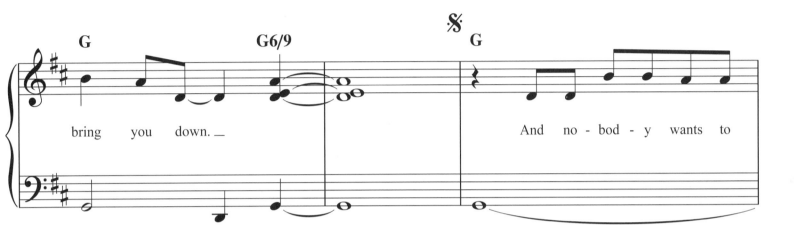

know you now, _ and no - bod - y wants to show you how. _____

_ So, if _____ you're lost _ and on _____ your own, you can

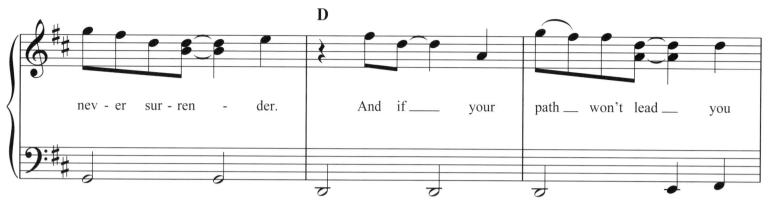

never sur-ren - der. And if ____ your path __ won't lead __ you

home, you can nev - er sur-ren - der. And when the

night is cold __ and dark, you can __ see, you can see __ light.

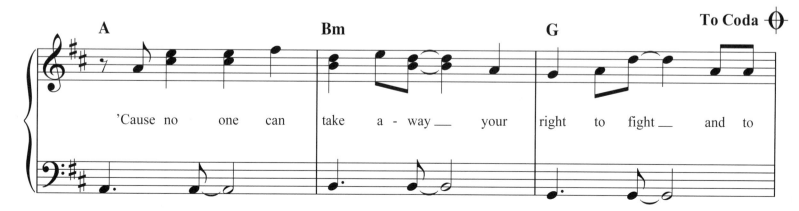

'Cause no one can take a - way __ your right to fight __ and to

D   Dsus2/F#

never sur - ren - der.

Gsus2   Dsus2

Dsus2/F#   Gsus2

D   F#m7   G

With a lit - tle per - se - ver - ance you ___ can get things done ___

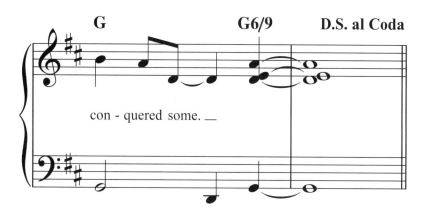

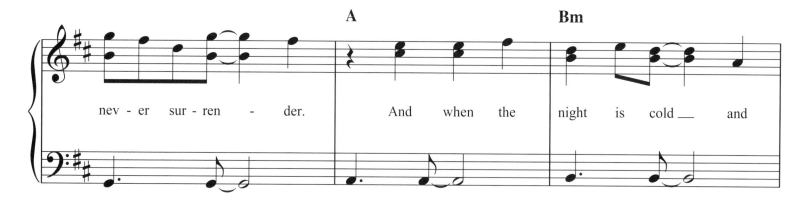

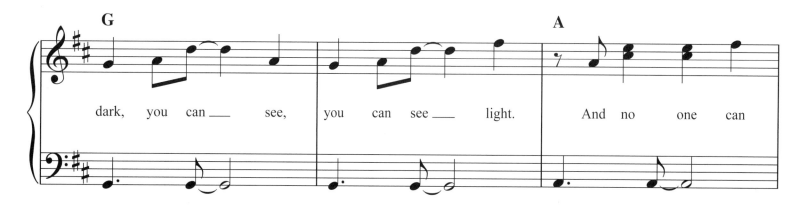

take a - way __ your right to fight __ and to nev - er sur - ren - der, to

nev - er sur - ren - der.

rit.

ROCK YOU LIKE A HURRICANE

Words and Music by RUDOLF SCHENKER,
KLAUS MEINE and HERMAN RAREBELL

Moderately fast

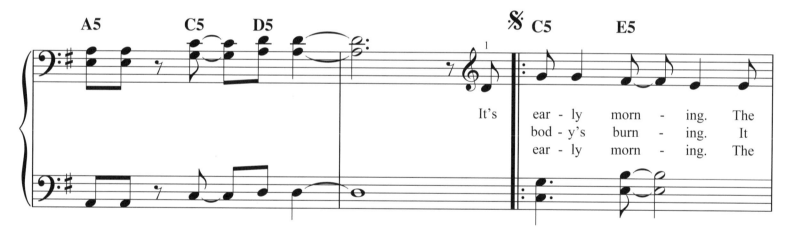

It's ear-ly morn-ing. The
bod-y's burn-ing. It
ear-ly morn-ing. The

sun comes out. ___ Last night was shak-ing and pret-ty loud. ___ My
starts to shout. ___ De-sire is com-ing. It breaks out loud. ___ Lust
sun comes out. ___ Last night was shak-ing and pret-ty loud. ___ My

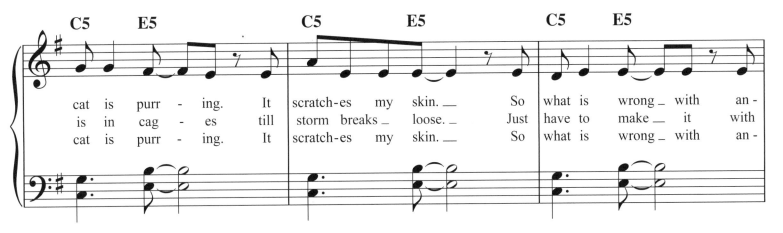

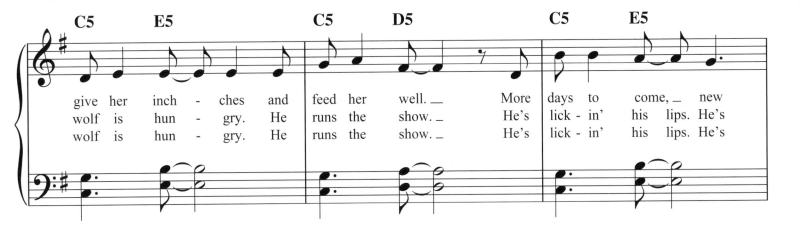

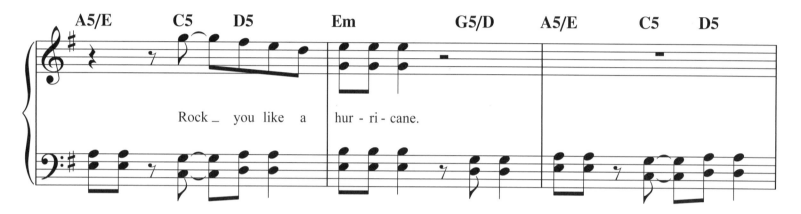

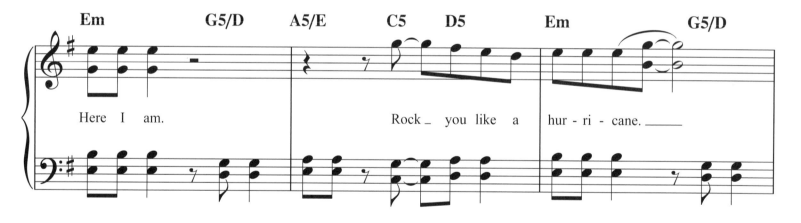

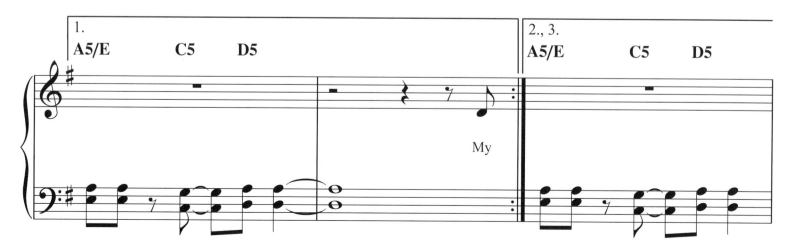

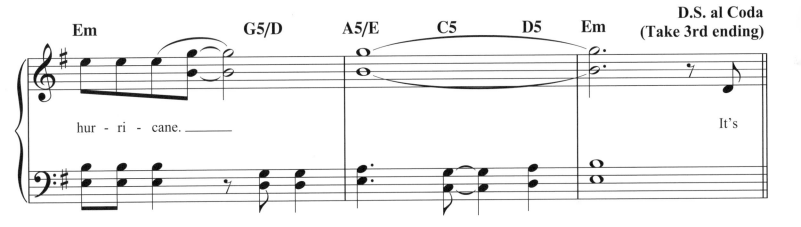

RUNAWAY

Words and Music by JON BON JOVI
and GEORGE KARAK

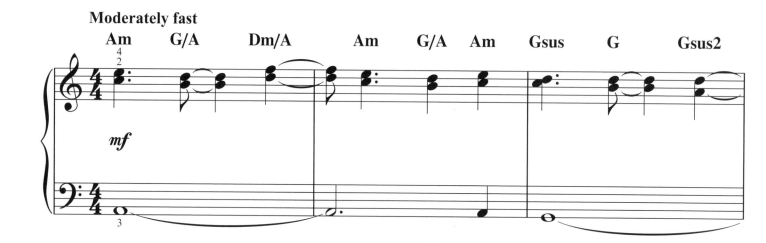

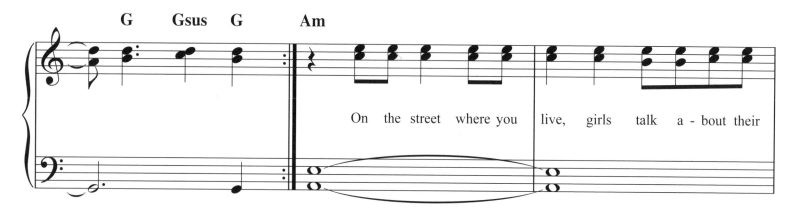

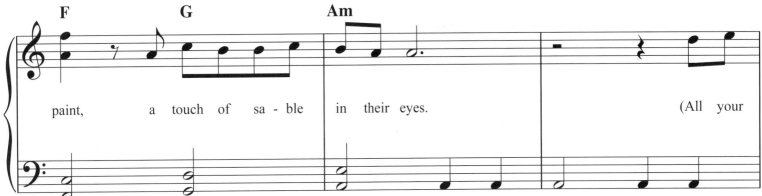

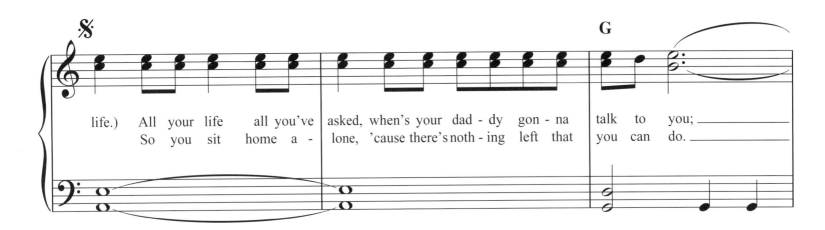

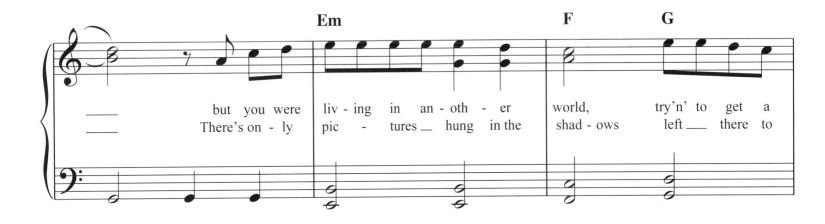

56

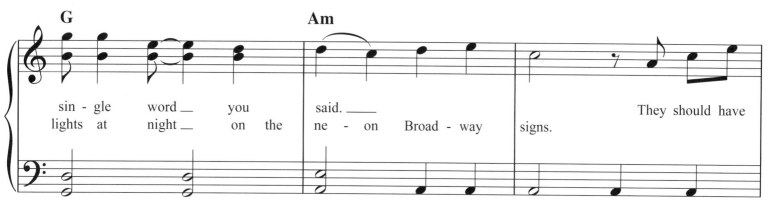

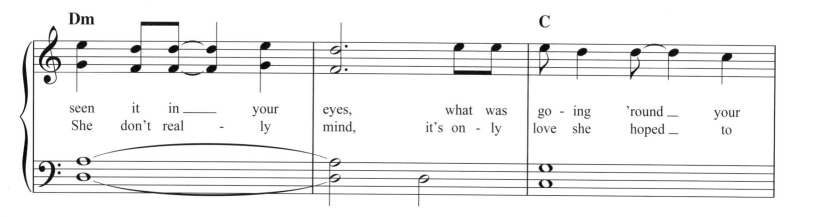

fast all ____ those things he could - n't say.

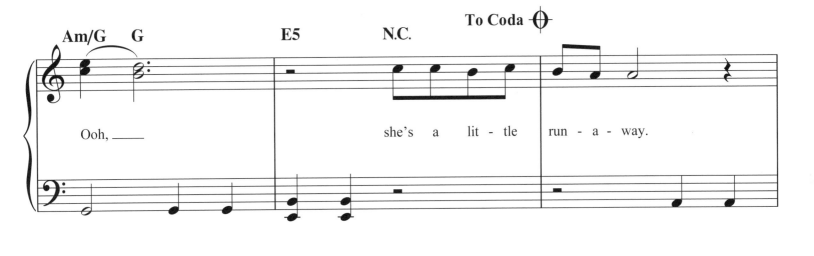

Ooh, ____ she's a lit - tle run - a - way.

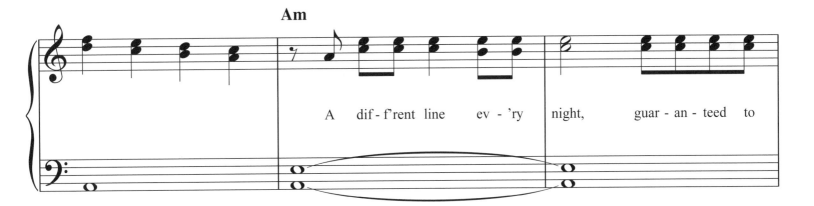

A dif - f'rent line ev - 'ry night, guar - an - teed to

blow your mind. I see you out on the

streets; call - ing for a wild __ time.

run - a- way. __

No one heard __ a

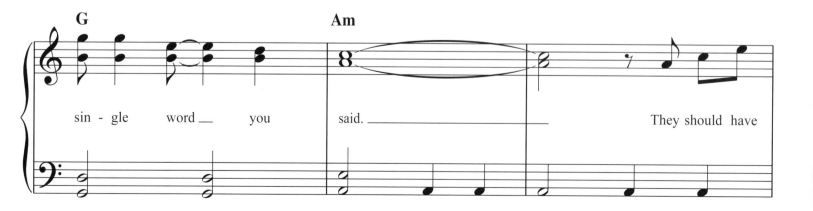

sin - gle word __ you said. _____ They should have

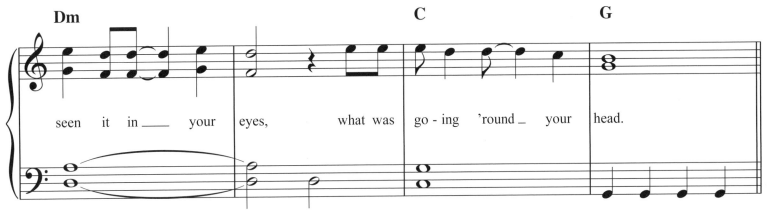

seen it in ___ your eyes, what was go - ing 'round __ your head.

Ooh, _____ she's a lit - tle run - a - way.
Ooh, _____ she's a lit - tle run - a - way.

Dad - dy's girl ___ learned fast all ___ those things he
Dad - dy's girl ___ learned fast; now ___ she works the

could - n't say.
night a - way.

RUNNING UP THAT HILL

Words and Music by
KATE BUSH

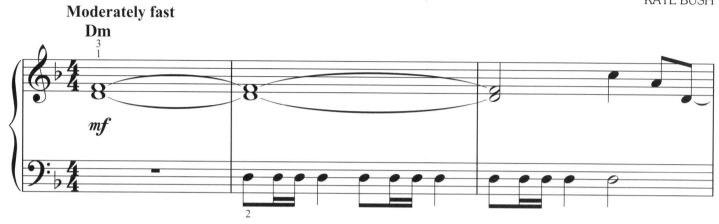

It does-n't hurt ____ me.

D'you wan-na feel ____ how it feels? ____

62

if I on-ly could, _ I'd make a deal with God _ and I'd get him to swap _ our plac-

- es. Be run-ning up that road, _ be run-ning up that hill, _ be run-ning up that build-

- ing. _____ See if I on-ly could, _

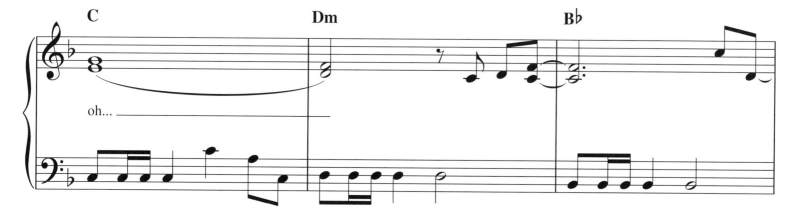

oh... _____

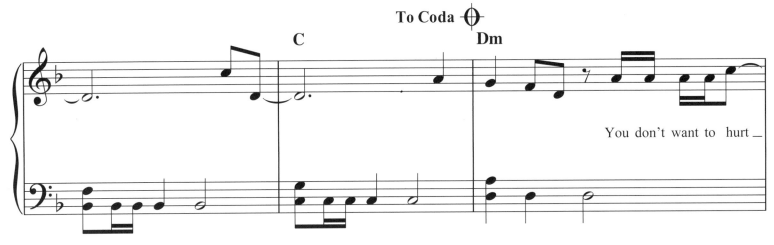

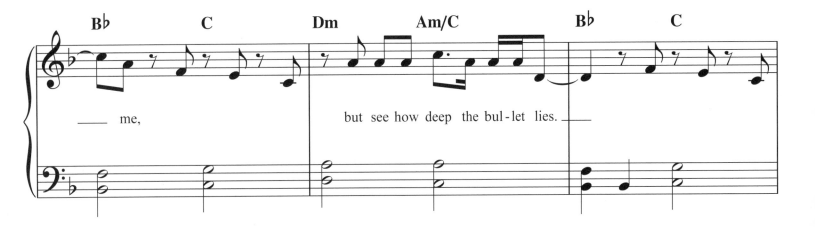

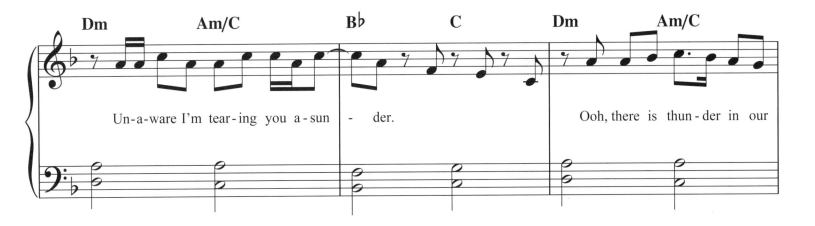

64

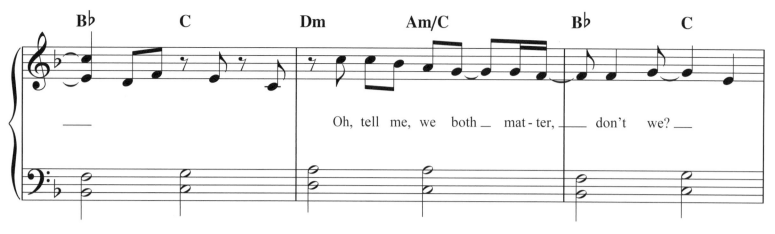

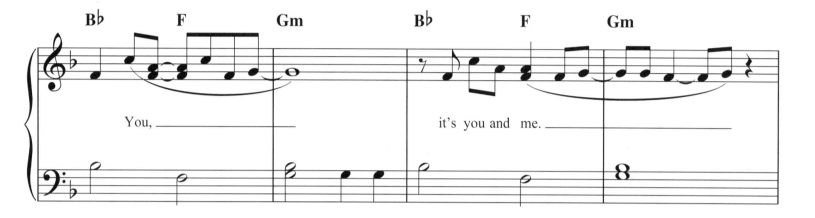

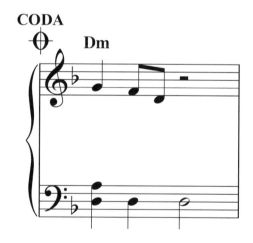

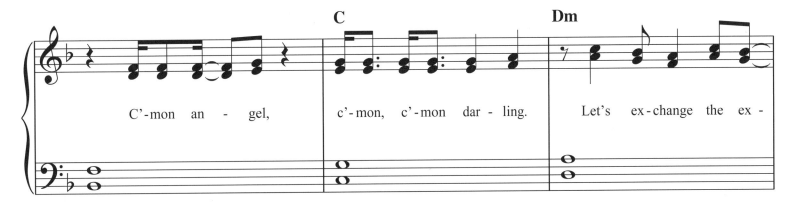

And if I on - ly could ___ I'd make a deal with God ___

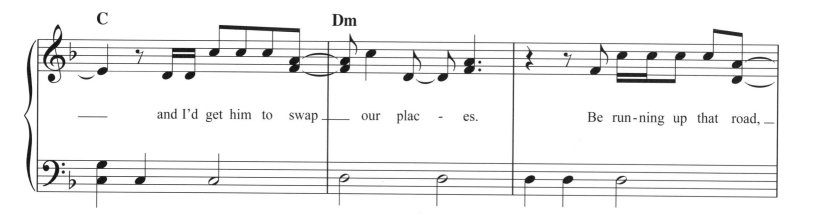

___ and I'd get him to swap ___ our plac - es. Be run - ning up that road, ___

___ be run - ning up that hill, ___ with no prob - lems. ___

Play 3 times

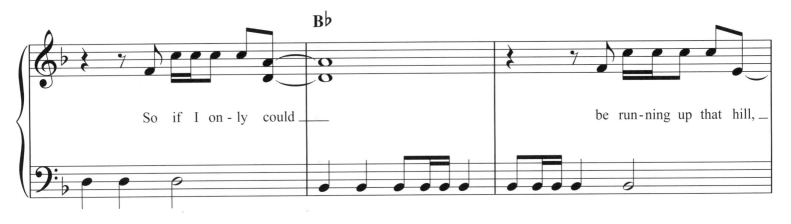

So if I on-ly could be run-ning up that hill,

with no prob - lems.

If I on - ly could, I'd be run-ning up that hill.

If I on - ly could, I'd be run-ning up that hill.

SEPARATE WAYS
(Worlds Apart)

Words and Music by STEVE PERRY
and JONATHAN CAIN

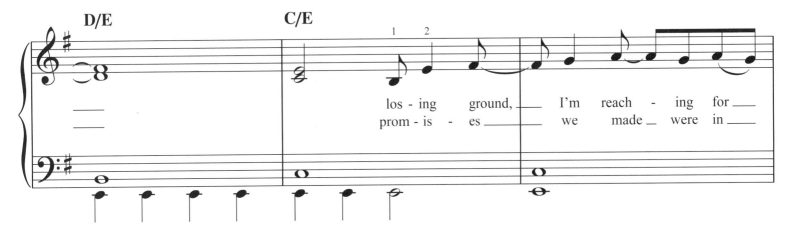

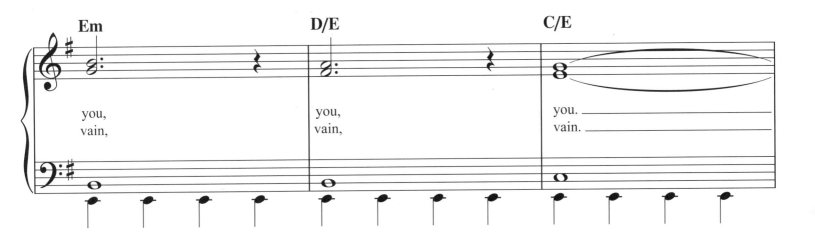

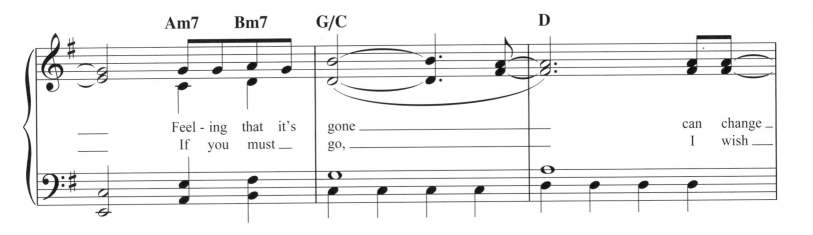

to sur - vive ____ the tide, ____ love ____ di - vides. ____
Take care ____ my love; ____ miss ____ you love. ____

Some - day love ____ will find you;

break those chains ____ that bind you. ____ One night will ____

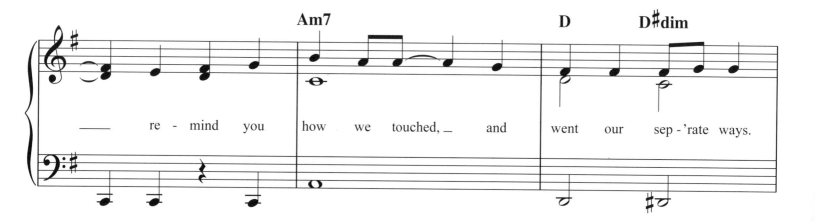

____ re - mind you how we touched, ____ and went our sep - 'rate ways.

If he ev - er hurts you, true love won't

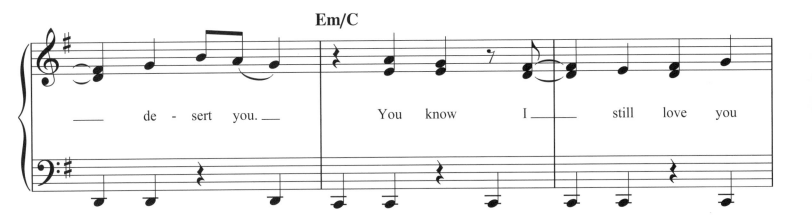

de - sert you. You know I still love you

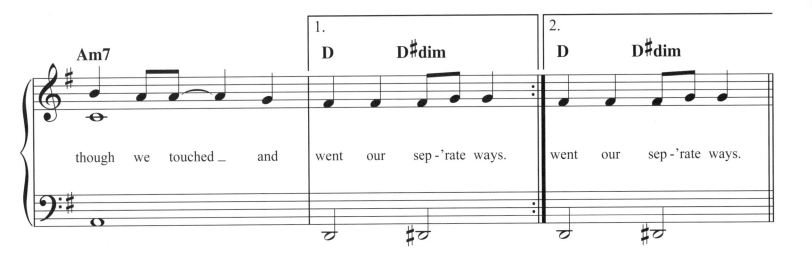

though we touched and went our sep -'rate ways. went our sep -'rate ways.

Some - day love will find you; break those chains

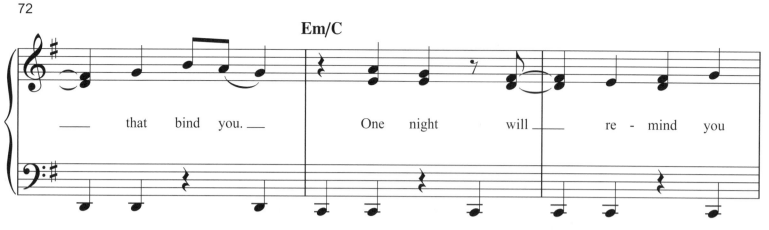

that bind you. ___ One night will ___ re - mind you

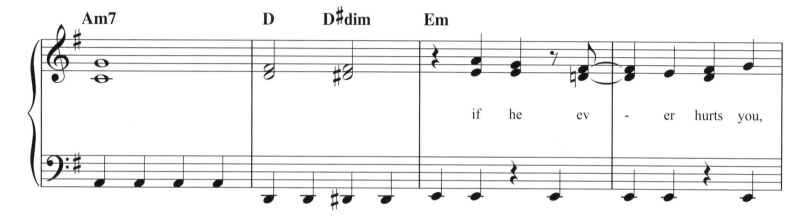

if he ev - er hurts you,

true love won't ___ de - sert you. ___ You know I ___

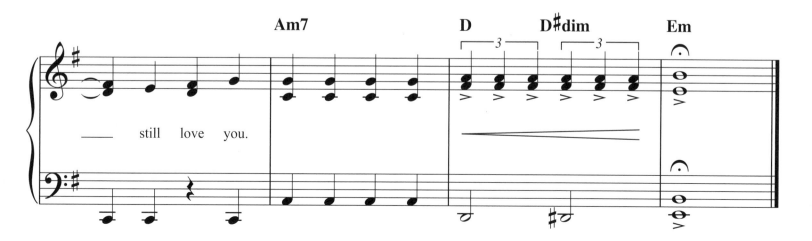

___ still love you.

TIME AFTER TIME

Words and Music by CYNDI LAUPER
and ROB HYMAN

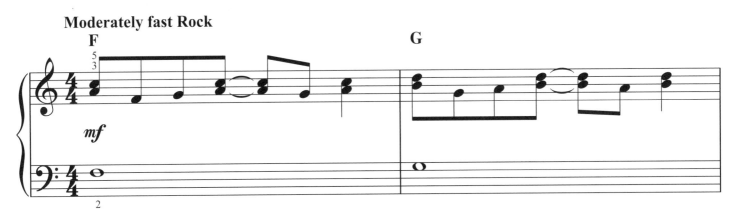

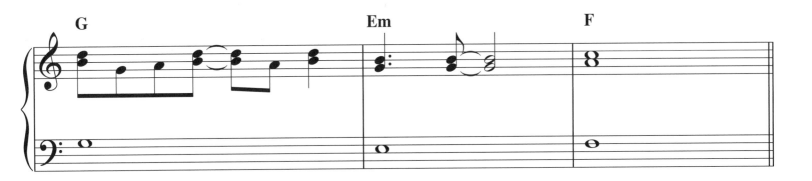

Ly - in' in ___ my bed I hear ___ the clock tick ___ and

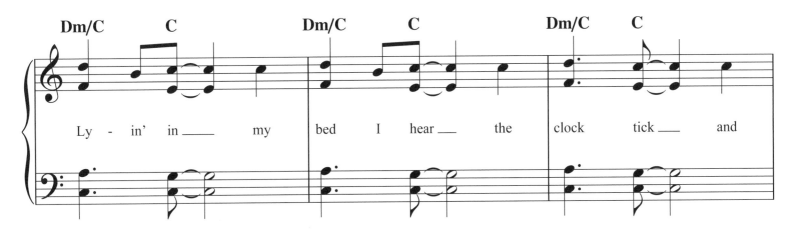

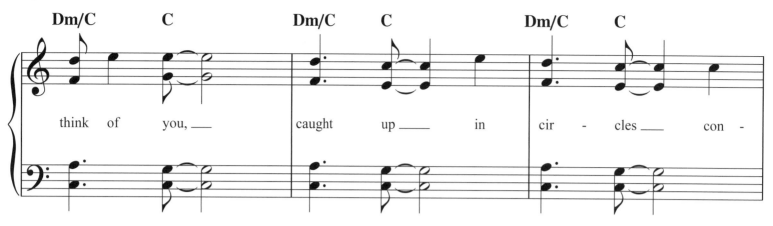

think of you, ____ caught up ____ in cir - cles ____ con -

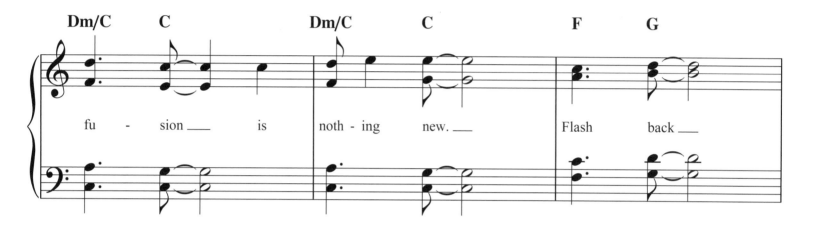

fu - sion ____ is noth - ing new. ____ Flash back ____

warm nights, _ al - most left ____ be - hind.

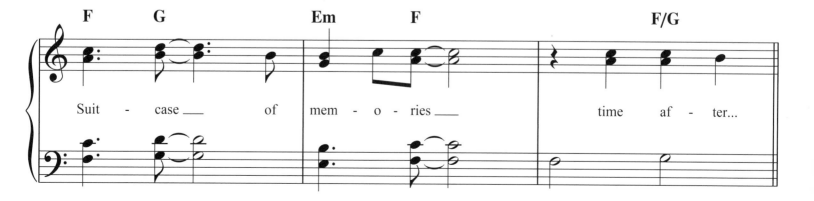

Suit - case ____ of mem - o - ries ____ time af - ter...

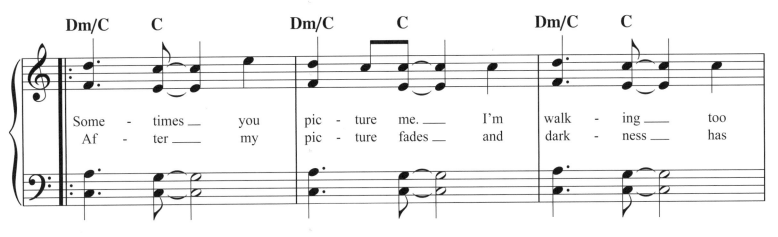

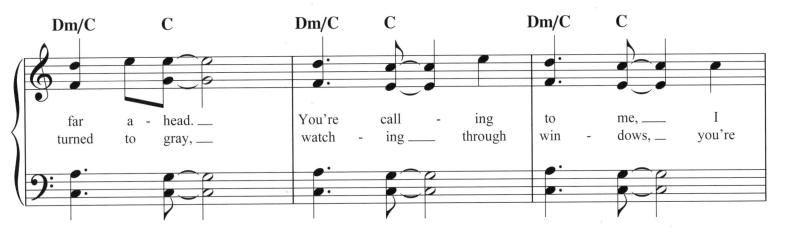

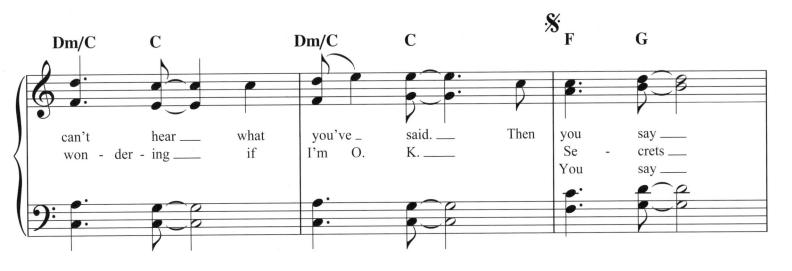

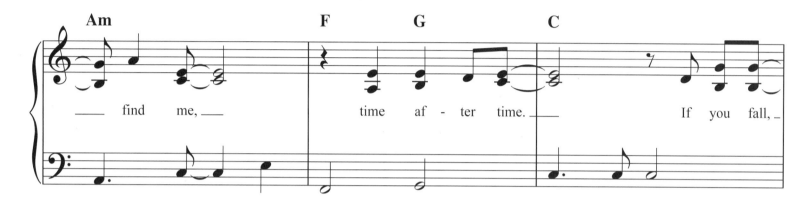

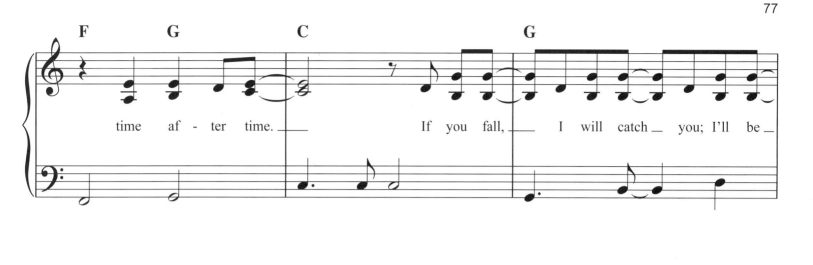

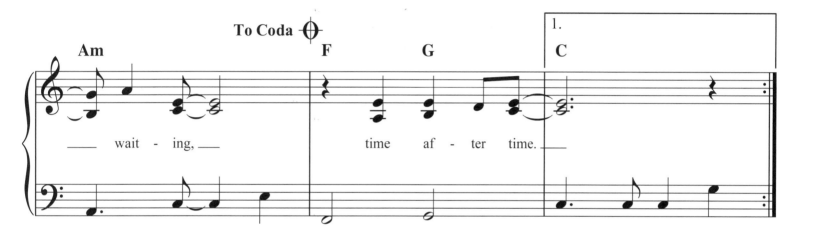

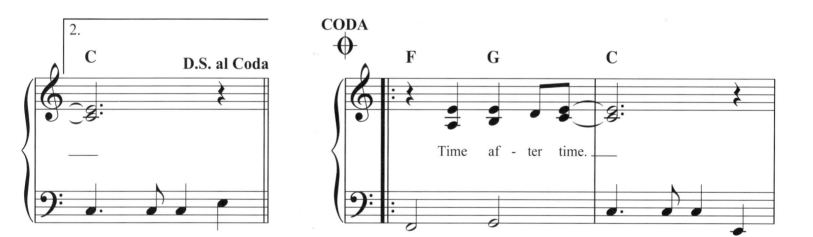

SHOULD I STAY OR SHOULD I GO

Words and Music by MICK JONES
and JOE STRUMMER

Dar-ling, you've got to let me know:
tease.
should I stay or should I
You're hap-py when I'm on my

go?
knees.
If you say that you are mine,
One day is fine and next is black.

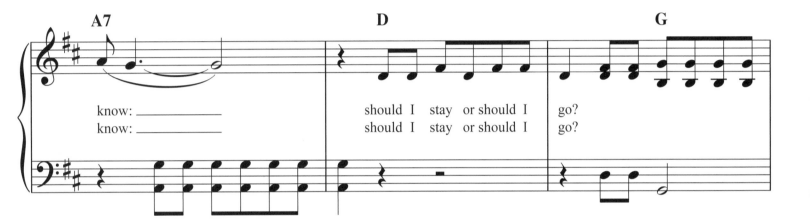

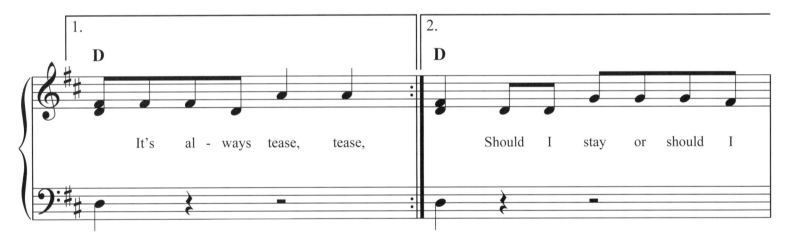

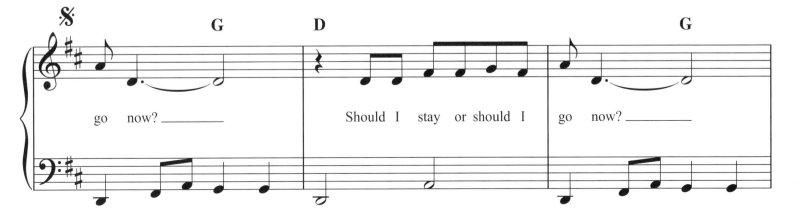

If I go there will be trou - ble. _____ And if I stay, it will be

dou - ble. _____ So come on and let me know. _____

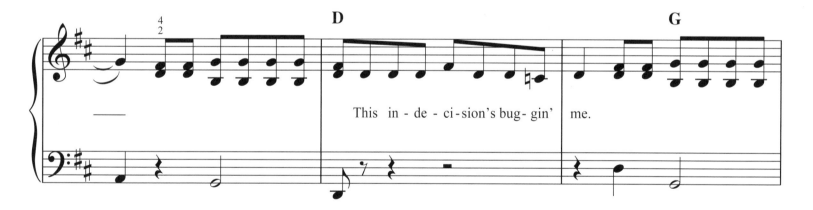

_____ This in - de - ci -sion's bug- gin' me.

If you don't want me, set me free. Ex - act - ly who'm I s'posed to

be? _____ Don't you know which clothes e - ven fit me?

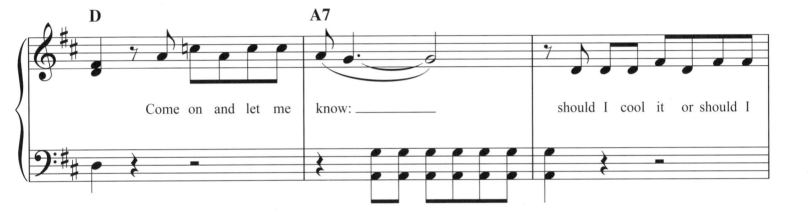

Come on and let me know: _____ should I cool it or should I

D.S. al Coda

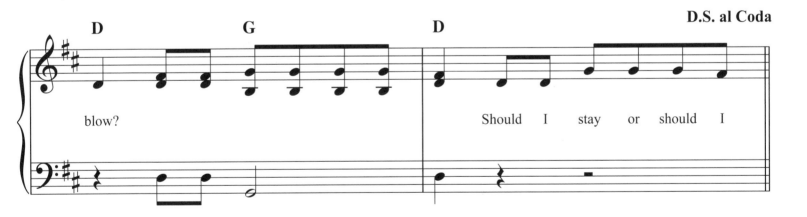

blow? Should I stay or should I

___ Should I stay or should I go?

STRANGER THINGS
MAIN TITLE THEME

By KYLE DIXON
and MICHAEL STEIN

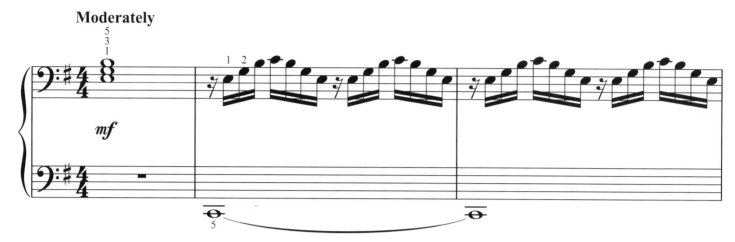

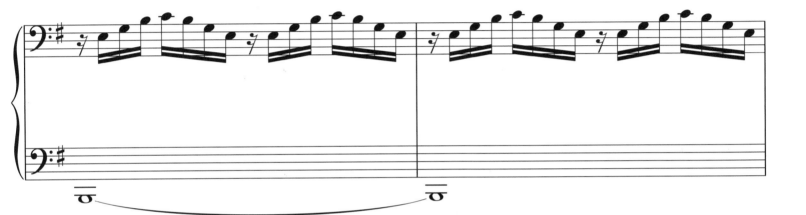

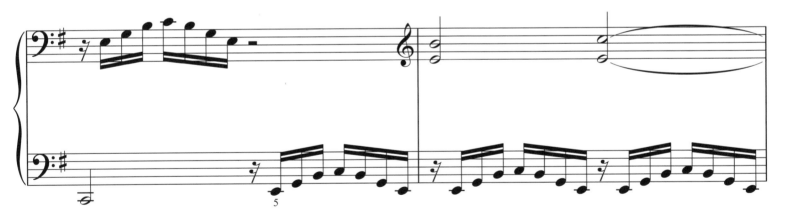

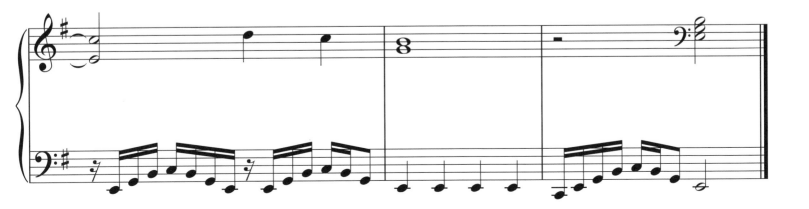

TALKING IN YOUR SLEEP

Words and Music by JIMMY MARINOS,
WALLY PALMAR, MIKE SKILL,
COZ CANLER and PETER SOLLEY

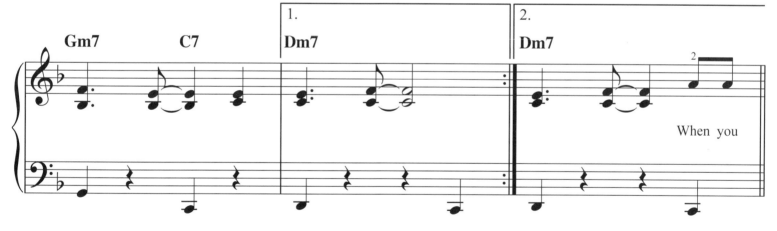

When you

close your eyes ___ and you go to sleep ___
hold you in ___ my arms at night ___

and it's down to the sound of a heart - beat
don't you know you're sleep - ing in a spot - light?

I can hear the things that you're
And all your dreams that you
close your eyes and you

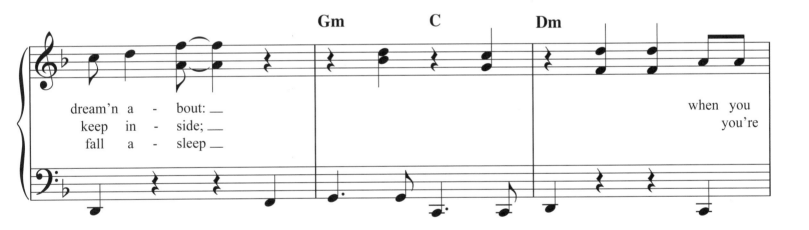

dream'n a - bout:
keep in - side;
fall a - sleep
when you
you're

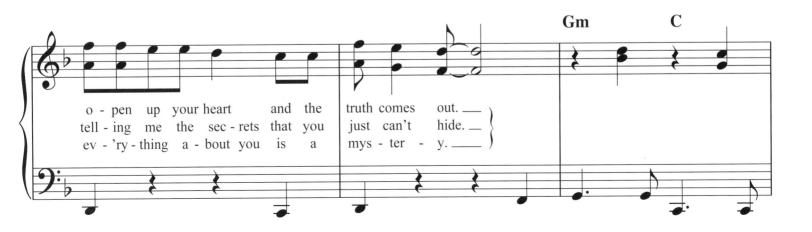

o - pen up your heart and the truth comes out.
tell - ing me the sec - rets that you just can't hide.
ev - 'ry - thing a - bout you is a mys - ter - y.

You tell me that you want me, you

tell me that you need me, you tell me that you love me.

And I know that I'm right, _ 'cause I hear it in the night. _____

I hear the sec-rets that you keep when you're

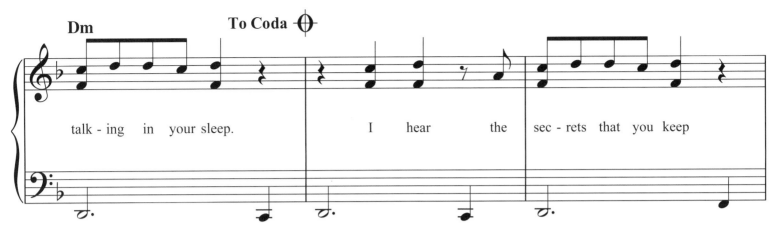

talk - ing in your sleep.   I hear the sec - rets that you keep

when you're talk-ing in your sleep. When I   talk-ing in your sleep. When you

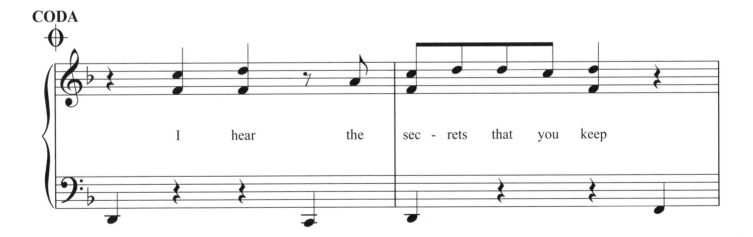

I   hear   the   sec - rets   that   you   keep

when you're   talk - ing   in   your   sleep.

YOU SPIN ME ROUND
(Like a Record)

Words and Music by PETER BURNS,
STEPHEN COY, MICHAEL PERCY
and TIM LEVER

Dance pop

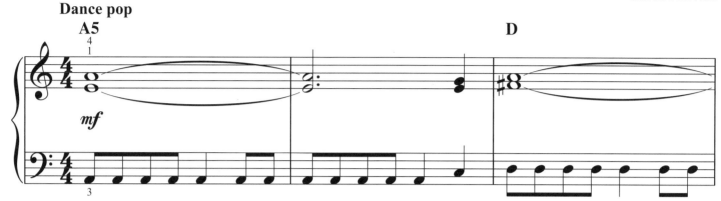

Yeah,
I,
I,
I,

I got to know your name.
I got my sights on you.
I got to be your friend.

Well, and
And
And

I
I,
I

could trace your pri-vate num - ber, ba - by.
I've got to have my way now, ba - by.
would like to move in just a lit-tle bit clos - er.

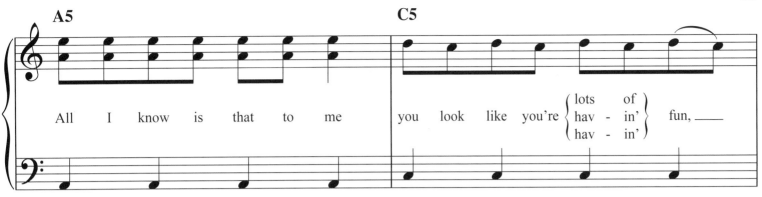

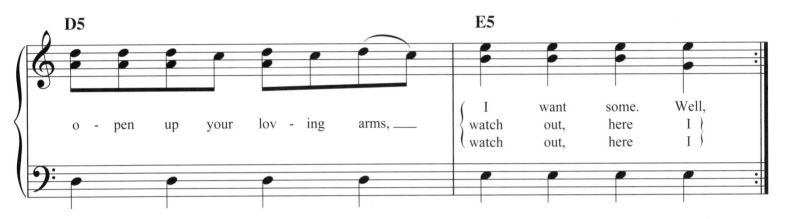

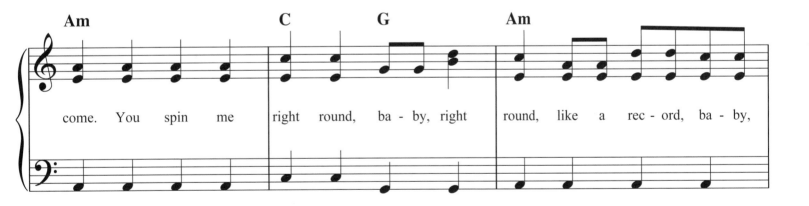

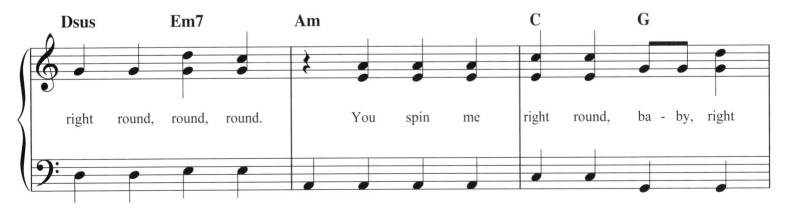

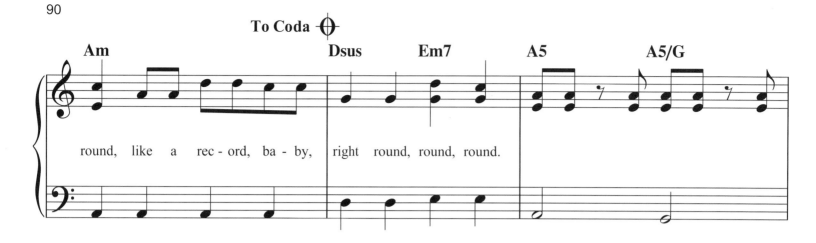

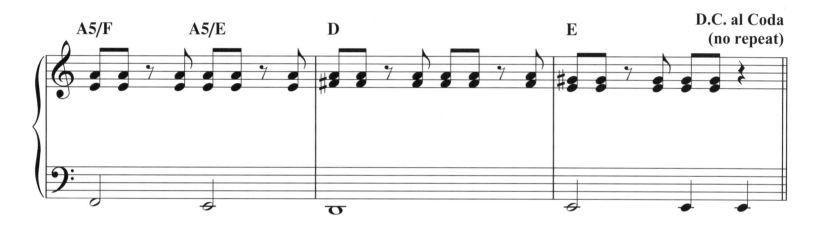

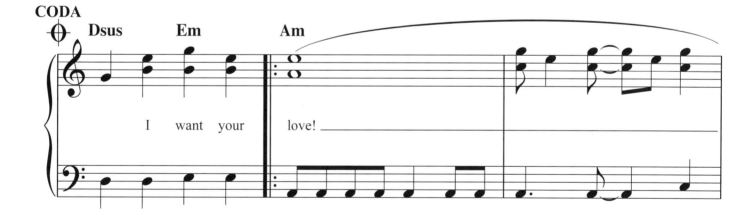

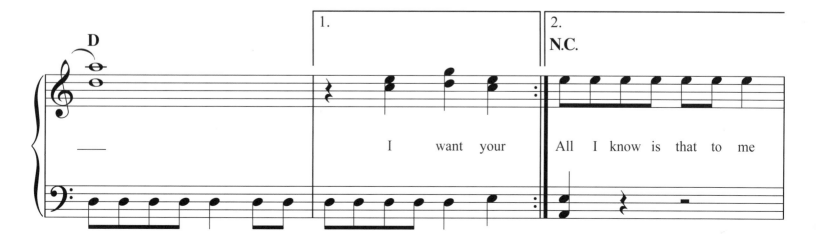

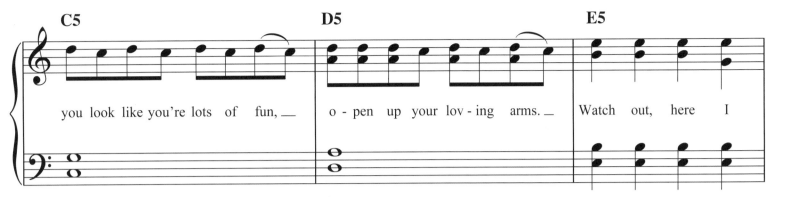

you look like you're lots of fun, __ o - pen up your lov - ing arms. __ Watch out, here I

come. You spin me right round, ba - by, right round, like a rec - ord, ba - by,

right round, round, round. You spin me right round, ba - by, right

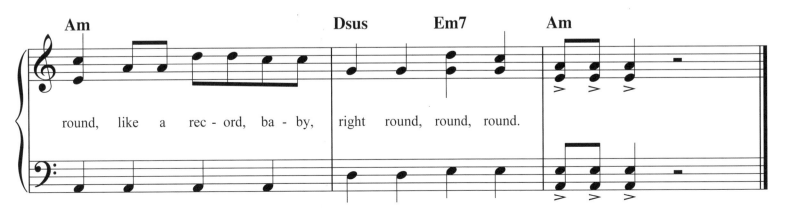

round, like a rec - ord, ba - by, right round, round, round.

WAKE ME UP BEFORE YOU GO-GO

Words and Music by
GEORGE MICHAEL

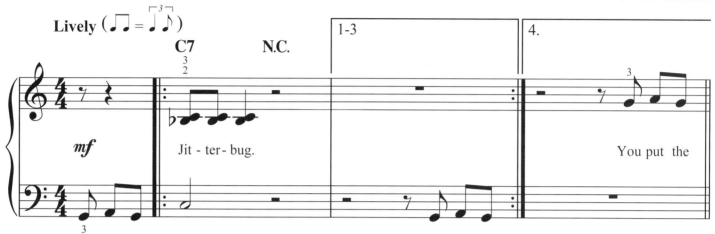

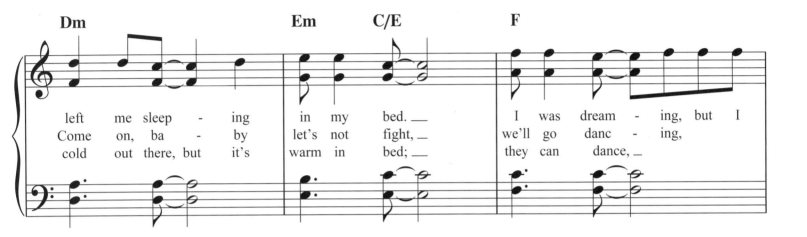

94

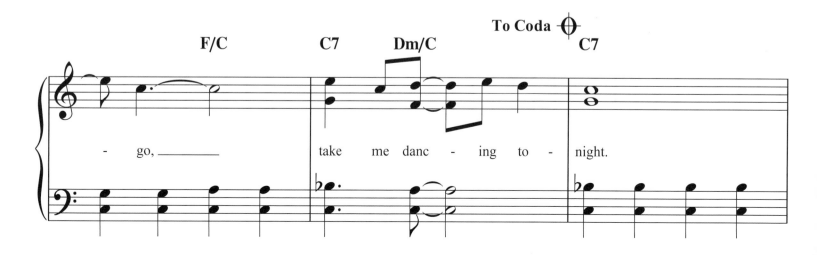

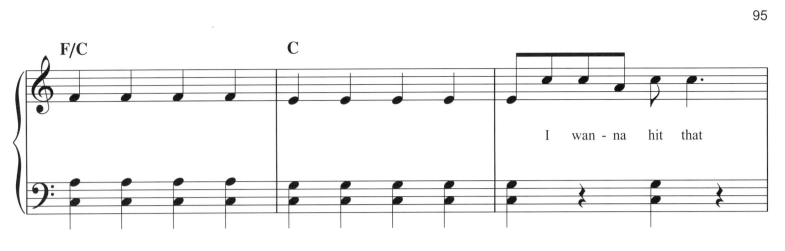

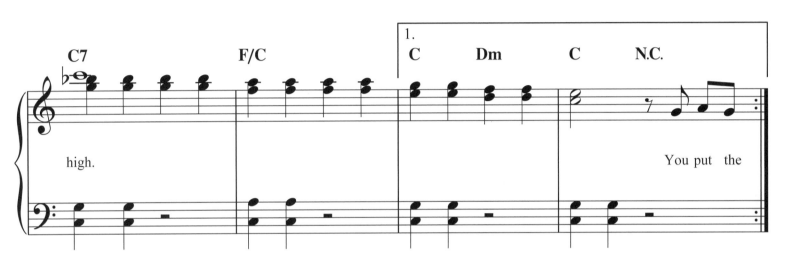

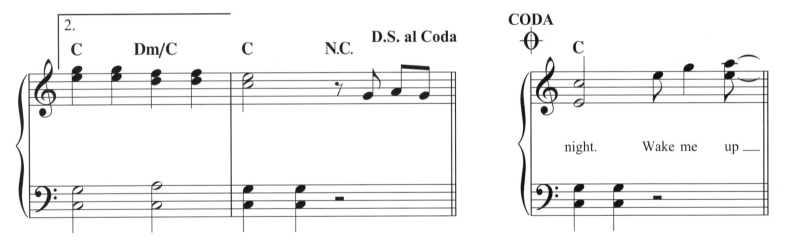

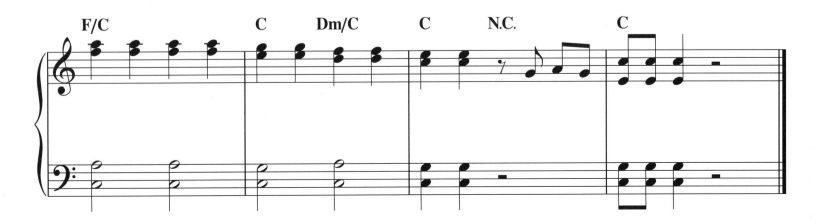